Math in Focus®

Singapore Math
by Marshall Cavendish

Implementation Guide

place value • regrouping • hundreds • tens • skip counting • measurement • mental math • graphs • ones • patterns •

Support for Planning and Instruction

2015 Edition

Printed in the U.S.A.

ISBN 978-0-544-19259-1

4 5 6 7 8 9 10 1689 24 23 22 21 20 19 18 17 16 15 14
4500463668 A B C D E F G

Contents

Teacher Tip:

Reading this section will help you understand the pedagogy of *Math in Focus.*

What is *Math in Focus* and Singapore Math?

Welcome to *Math in Focus®: Singapore Math* by Marshall Cavendish. This guide is intended to help you get started implementing *Math in Focus* in your classroom. As you work through the guide, you'll develop an understanding of the resources available to you in the *Math in Focus* program.

Math In Focus is the United States edition of the most widely used curriculum in Singapore, which has consistently been the top-performing country in international assessments such as TIMSS and PISA. Because Singapore has been so consistently successful in math, its curriculum was one of the main models used to write the Common Core State Standards. Singapore Math helped to shape not only the content of the Common Core State Standards but also especially the philosophy and pedagogy.

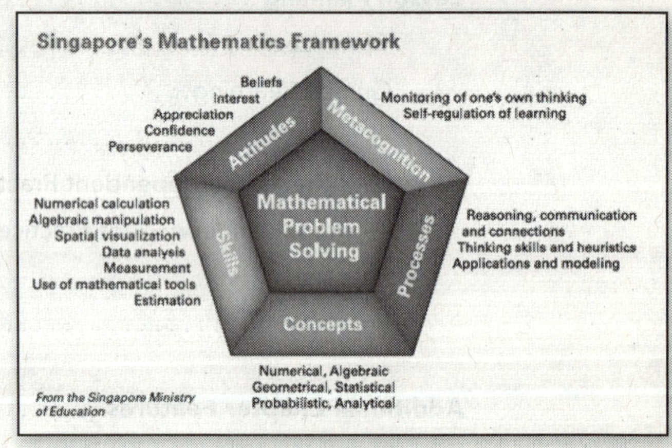

Before we get started, we want you to understand the underlying premise of Singapore Math that is represented in this pentagon. This is the Mathematics Framework from the Ministry of Education in Singapore.

- Problem solving is at the heart of any math program—you learn math to solve problems.
- You must possess the conceptual base to understand and solve problems.
- You must possess the relevant skills and understand the processes involved in problem solving.
- You must possess metacognition—the understanding of your learning processes.
- Finally, you must possess confidence and persistence to be a successful problem solver.

Program Components

Teacher Tip:

At first, all you will need is the Teacher's Edition. Later, you can look at all the ancillary materials.

Math in Focus Components for Grades 1–5:

- **Teacher's Edition A and B.**
- **Student Book A and B** are hard cover, non-consumable books that students use every day. Book A focuses primarily on number and operation, while the primary focus of Book B is geometry and measurement.
- **Workbooks A and B** are consumable books that provide independent practice both in school and at home. The work is assigned when students demonstrate they can do the problems independently.
- **Reteach A and B, Extra Practice A and B, and Enrichment A and B** provide material for differentiation. The books come as Blackline masters, and the material is also available online.
- **Assessments** are available as Blackline masters and online. They include pre- and post- chapter tests as well as cumulative, semester, and year-end assessments. There are two versions for the chapter tests: one in the Student Book or Workbook and one in the Assessments book.
- **School-to-Home Connections** provides a newsletter for each chapter to be sent home to facilitate communication with families. They contain "at home" activities that align with the chapters in *Math in Focus*.
- **Manipulative Kits** are an integral part of *Math in Focus*. Manipulative kits are available in three different sizes to supply all your needs or to supplement previously purchased materials.
- **Virtual Manipulatives** are also an integral part of *Math in Focus* and are available online.
- **Teacher's Guide to Transition** provides online support to transition with fidelity to the Math in Focus program.
- **Achieving Facts Fluency** offers activities and worksheets to build computational fluency.

Getting Started

Teacher Tip:

Use sticky notes, tabs, and if allowed, a highlighter to take notes right in your Teacher's Edition. You may want to find all the planning pieces listed here before you go further in this guide.

How to Plan a Chapter and a Lesson

One benefit of the *Math in Focus* curriculum is that while it includes many different activities and instructional practices, the structure of each grade level and each chapter is the same. Once you learn this structure, you will find it quite easy to plan your lessons.

As you plan to teach each chapter and its lessons, we suggest you work through the parts of each chapter and lesson in the following order:

- Scope and Sequence
- Common Core and Singapore Pathways
- Chapter Overview
- Chapter Wrap Up
- Chapter Review/Test
- Chapter Planning Guide
- Chapter Introduction
- Recall Prior Knowledge and Quick Check
- Teacher's Guide to Transition
- Lesson Planning
  - Teach/Learn
  - Guided Learning
  - Let's Practice
  - Workbook
  - Reteach
  - Enrichment
- Put on Your Thinking Cap! and Math Journal
- Assessment

Refer to your Teacher's Edition as we work through each of these elements.

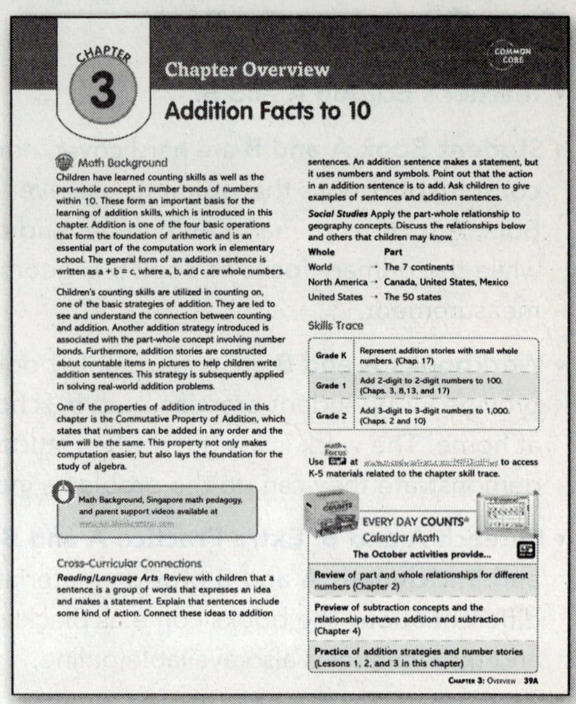

CHAPTER 3

Chapter Overview

Addition Facts to 10

Math Background

Children have learned counting skills as well as the part-whole concept in number bonds of numbers within 10. These form an important basis for the learning of addition skills, which is introduced in this chapter. Addition is one of the four basic operations that form the foundation of arithmetic and is an essential part of the computation work in elementary school. The general form of an addition sentence is written as a + b = c, where a, b, and c are whole numbers.

Children's counting skills are utilized in counting on, one of the basic strategies of addition. They are led to see and understand the connection between counting and addition. Another addition strategy introduced is associated with the part-whole concept involving number bonds. Furthermore, addition stories are constructed about countable items in pictures to help children write addition sentences. This strategy is subsequently applied in solving real-world addition problems.

One of the properties of addition introduced in this chapter is the Commutative Property of Addition, which states that numbers can be added in any order and the sum will be the same. This property not only makes computation easier, but also lays the foundation for the study of algebra.

Math Background, Singapore math pedagogy, and parent support videos available at

Cross-Curricular Connections

Reading/Language Arts Review with children that a sentence is a group of words that expresses an idea and makes a statement. Explain that sentences include some kind of action. Connect these ideas to addition sentences. An addition sentence makes a statement, but it uses numbers and symbols. Point out that the action in an addition sentence is to add. Ask children to give examples of sentences and addition sentences.

Social Studies Apply the part-whole relationship to geography concepts. Discuss the relationships below and others that children may know.

Whole		Part
World	→	The 7 continents
North America	→	Canada, United States, Mexico
United States	→	The 50 states

Skills Trace

Grade K	Represent addition stories with small whole numbers. (Chap. 17)
Grade 1	Add 2-digit to 2-digit numbers to 100. (Chaps. 3, 8,13, and 17)
Grade 2	Add 3-digit to 3-digit numbers to 1,000. (Chaps. 2 and 10)

Use Math in Focus at to access K-5 materials related to the chapter skill trace.

EVERY DAY COUNTS® Calendar Math

The October activities provide...

Review of part and whole relationships for different numbers (Chapter 2)

Preview of subtraction concepts and the relationship between addition and subtraction (Chapter 4)

Practice of addition strategies and number stories (Lessons 1, 2, and 3 in this chapter)

CHAPTER 3: OVERVIEW 39A

Grade 1 is shown as an example.

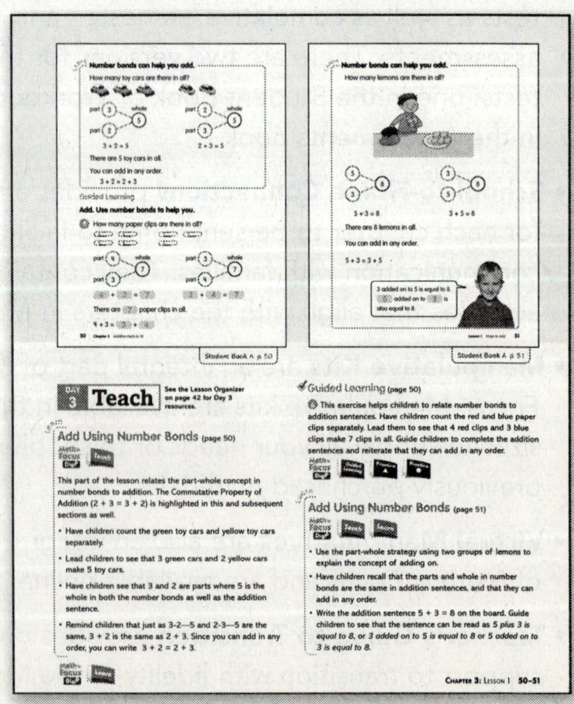

Number bonds can help you add.

How many toy cars are there in all?

3 + 2 = 5 2 + 3 = 5

There are 5 toy cars in all.

You can add in any order.

3 + 2 = 2 + 3

Guided Learning

Add. Use number bonds to help you.

How many paper clips are there in all?

There are paper clips in all.

4 + 3 = +

Student Book A p. 50

Number bonds can help you add.

How many lemons are there in all?

5 + 3 = 8 3 + 5 = 8

There are 8 lemons in all.

You can add in any order.

5 + 3 = 3 + 5

3 added on to 5 is equal to 8. added on to is also equal to 8.

Student Book A p. 51

DAY 3 Teach — See the Lesson Organizer on page 42 for Day 3 resources.

Add Using Number Bonds (page 50)

This part of the lesson relates the part-whole concept in number bonds to addition. The Commutative Property of Addition (2 + 3 = 3 + 2) is highlighted in this and subsequent sections as well.

- Have children count the green toy cars and yellow toy cars separately.
- Lead children to see that 3 green cars and 2 yellow cars make 5 toy cars.
- Have children see that 3 and 2 are parts where 5 is the whole in both the number bonds as well as the addition sentence.
- Remind children that just as 3-2—5 and 2-3—5 are the same, 3 + 2 is the same as 2 + 3. Since you can add in any order, you can write 3 + 2 = 2 + 3.

Guided Learning (page 50)

This exercise helps children to relate number bonds to addition sentences. Have children count the red and blue paper clips separately. Lead them to see that 4 red clips and 3 blue clips make 7 clips in all. Guide children to complete the addition sentences and reiterate that they can add in any order.

Add Using Number Bonds (page 51)

- Use the part-whole strategy using two groups of lemons to explain the concept of adding on.
- Have children recall that the parts and whole in number bonds are the same in addition sentences, and that they can add in any order.
- Write the addition sentence 5 + 3 = 8 on the board. Guide children to see that the sentence can be read as *5 plus 3 is equal to 8*, or *3 added on to 5 is equal to 8* or *5 added on to 3 is equal to 8.*

CHAPTER 3: LESSON 1 50–51

Grade 1 is shown as an example.

Chapter Planning

Teacher Tip:

The Common Core and Singapore Pathway charts appear in Teacher's Edition Book A

Scope and Sequence

Before you begin planning the first chapter, you will probably want to know the sequence of topics you will be teaching this year, especially because it may differ from sequences you've used previously. In particular, as you look at the Table of Contents for Book A and Book B, you will see that many arithmetic topics are taught early in the school year and that these are followed with geometry and measurement topics.

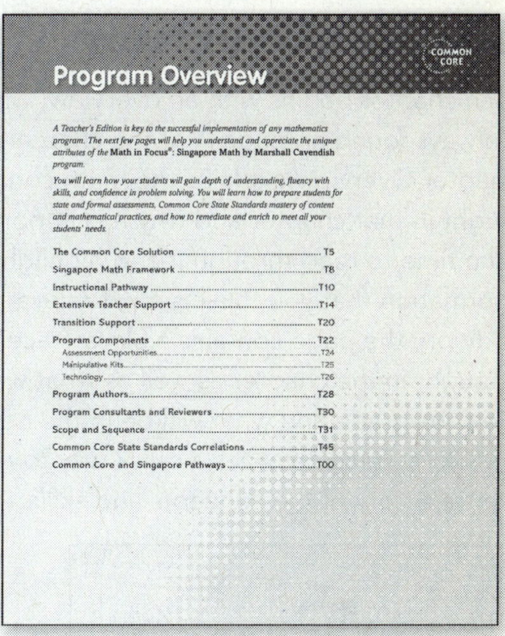

Program Overview

A Teacher's Edition is key to the successful implementation of any mathematics program. The next few pages will help you understand and appreciate the unique attributes of the **Math in Focus®: Singapore Math by Marshall Cavendish** *program.*

You will learn how your students will gain depth of understanding, fluency with skills, and confidence in problem solving. You will learn how to prepare students for state and formal assessments. Common Core State Standards mastery of content and mathematical practices, and how to remediate and enrich to meet all your students' needs.

After reviewing the Table of Contents, turn to the Scope and Sequence table in Teacher's Edition A. On these pages you'll see the scope of the topics in your grade as well as what has been taught in the previous grade and what will be taught in the next grade. Of course you will want to look in particular at the content of the chapter you are teaching, but these pages will also give you a general idea of all the content you will be teaching this year.

Common Core and Singapore Pathways

Also prior to planning for the first chapter you will want to turn to the Common Core and Singapore Pathways chart and choose whether to follow the Common Core or Singapore curriculum. The pathway provides a clear and concise plan for teaching the Common Core standards for the year. The pathway also shows the plan for the traditional Singapore math curriculum for the year. Toward the end of the school year you might decide to enrich students' learning by presenting select content from the pathway not chosen.

Grade 3 is shown as an example.

Teacher Tip:

Highlight the math information you think most relevant, keeping in mind where it is leading as students move forward.

Chapter Overview

Each chapter begins with an overview, which is always found on page A of the chapter. The Chapter Overview explains the math concept taught in that chapter and why it is important. Take time to read through it and highlight any information that you think is most relevant. In addition, the page contains a Skills Trace for what is taught in the chapter as well as what was in the previous grade and what will be in the next grade. The Skills Trace provides a quick way to recognize the trajectory of the concepts and skills.

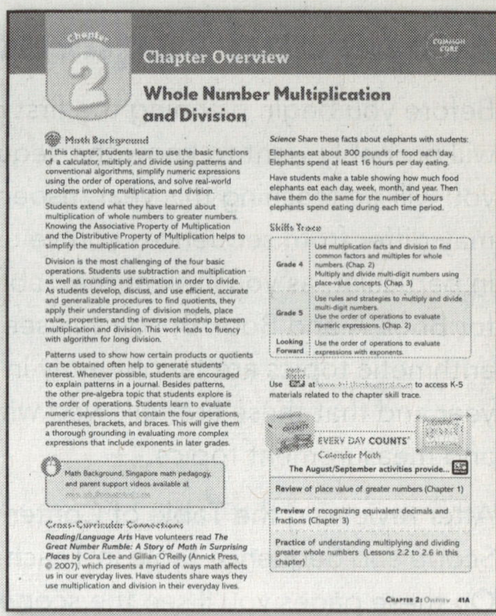

Grade 5 is shown as an example.

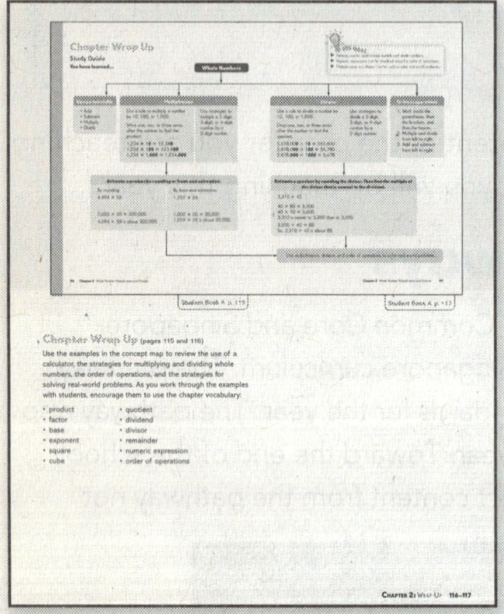

Grade 5 is shown as an example.

Chapter Wrap Up

The Chapter Wrap Up appears on the last page of every chapter, just before the Chapter Review/Test. It can also be found in the Student Book. The visual organizer in the Chapter Wrap Up provides an easy way to see what is taught in the chapter and the order it is presented in.

Chapter Review/Test

Use the chapter test from the Assessments book, which is also shown in tiny print in the Teacher's Edition at the end of each chapter. Working backwards from the chapter test will make your planning easier. By studying or taking the test, you will have an excellent idea of what will be expected of your students as well as the complexity of the assessed formats. (For example, for first graders, asking what is 3 more than 5 is more complex than asking what is 5 + 3.)

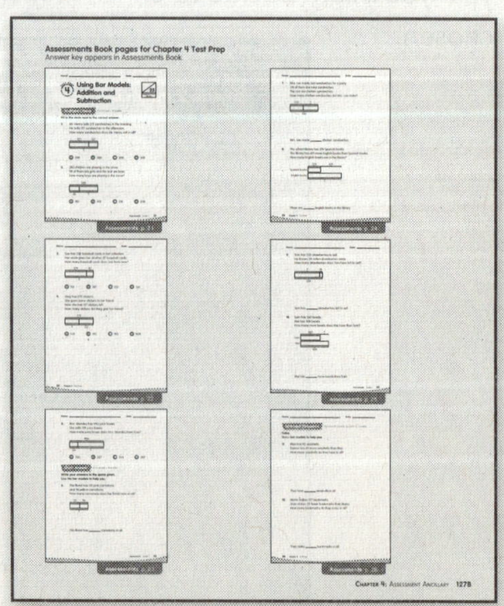

Grade 2 is shown as an example.

Chapter Planning Guide

The Chapter Planning Guide, which begins on page D of each chapter, is the best place to see how the chapter is laid out into lessons. Notice that some lessons require only one day, while others need two or three days. In the Chapter Planning Guide, you will see the teaching sequence of concepts, the length of time ideally expected, the objectives and vocabulary for each lesson, the printed materials available to you to teach the lesson, the necessary manipulatives, and the connection to the Common Core State Standards.

Take special note of two features as you look at these pages. First, notice all the lessons in a chapter focus on one big idea or concept. Next notice how carefully the lessons are sequenced. Each lesson logically flows from the previous one. Students first develop an understanding of the concept, then develop more efficient and more abstract understanding.

For example, in grades 2–5 the first chapter is about place value. The first lesson uses a concrete material such as base-ten materials or place-value chips to ensure that students can count, read, and write numbers. The second lesson introduces the place-value chart, which is used in every grade, as well as writing numbers in standard and expanded form. Students learn to compare numbers in the next lesson, and finally the last lesson focuses on finding place-value patterns.

Teacher Tip:

The first year that you use *Math in Focus*, it might take longer to complete a chapter because students may not have sufficient background knowledge. Figure on anywhere from 1–3 days extra for more difficult chapters.

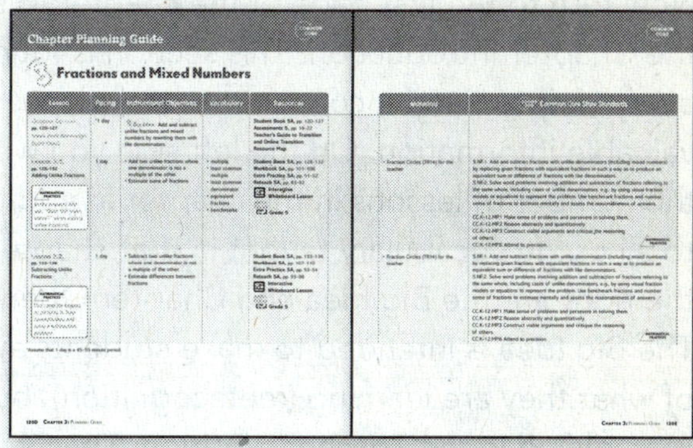

Grade 5 is shown as an example.

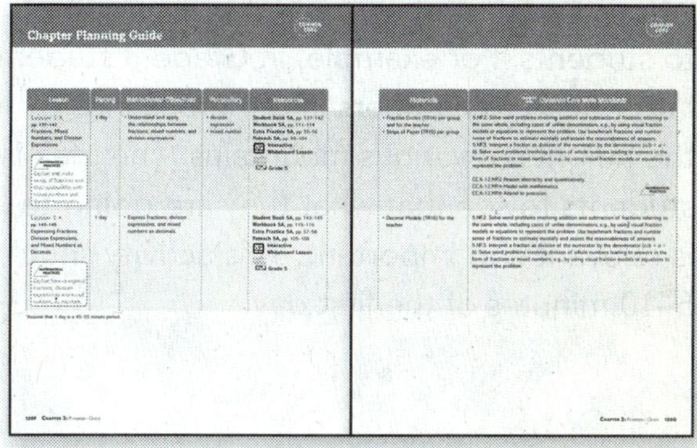

Grade 5 is shown as an example.

Teacher Tip:

Plan ahead for how you will teach the vocabulary. Will you use a word wall? How will you display vocabulary? Will students keep their own lists as well?

Chapter Introduction

Now turn to the first page of the chapter to see the Chapter Introduction. This section is found in every chapter, and it contains several pieces of valuable information. On the left side you will see the number of lessons in the chapter in addition to all of the vocabulary taught in that chapter. To the right are the Big Idea and Chapter Opener. The Big Idea is intended to make students aware of what they are learning (metacognition), but it is amplified in the Teacher's Edition. The Chapter Opener will help you introduce the new chapter to your students, providing context for the new topic. You may prefer to use a different context, but you do need some way of introducing the topic to students. For example, in Grade 3 students are introduced to numbers in the thousands by listing the heights of various mountains. The idea is for students to see that what they are going to learn is relevant and important. This activity should take 5–10 minutes of the first day.

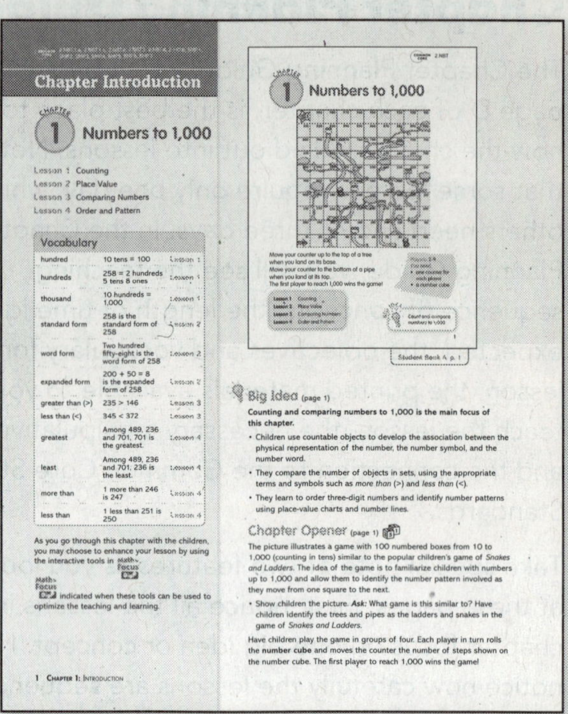

Chapter Introduction

Chapter 1 Numbers to 1,000

Lesson 1 Counting
Lesson 2 Place Value
Lesson 3 Comparing Numbers
Lesson 4 Order and Pattern

Vocabulary		
hundred	10 tens = 100	Lesson 1
hundreds	258 = 2 hundreds 5 tens 8 ones	Lesson 1
thousand	10 hundreds = 1,000	Lesson 1
standard form	258 is the standard form of 258	Lesson 2
word form	Two hundred fifty-eight is the word form of 258	Lesson 2
expanded form	200 + 50 = 8 is the expanded form of 258	Lesson 2
greater than (>)	235 > 146	Lesson 3
less than (<)	345 < 372	Lesson 3
greatest	Among 489, 236 and 701, 701 is the greatest.	Lesson 4
least	Among 489, 236 and 701, 236 is the least.	Lesson 4
more than	1 more than 246 is 247	Lesson 4
less than	1 less than 251 is 250	Lesson 4

As you go through this chapter with the children, you may choose to enhance your lesson by using the interactive tools in Math in Focus. Math in Focus indicated when these tools can be used to optimize the teaching and learning.

Student Book A p. 1

Big Idea (page 1)

Counting and comparing numbers to 1,000 is the main focus of this chapter.

- Children use countable objects to develop the association between the physical representation of the number, the number symbol, and the number word.
- They compare the number of objects in sets, using the appropriate terms and symbols such as *more than* (>) and *less than* (<).
- They learn to order three-digit numbers and identify number patterns using place-value charts and number lines.

Chapter Opener (page 1)

The picture illustrates a game with 100 numbered boxes from 10 to 1,000 (counting in tens) similar to the popular children's game of *Snakes and Ladders*. The idea of the game is to familiarize children with numbers up to 1,000 and allow them to identify the number pattern involved as they move from one square to the next.

- Show children the picture. ***Ask:*** What game is this similar to? Have children identify the trees and pipes as the ladders and snakes in the game of *Snakes and Ladders*.

Have children play the game in groups of four. Each player in turn rolls the **number cube** and moves the counter the number of steps shown on the number cube. The first player to reach 1,000 wins the game!

1 Chapter 1: Introduction

Grade 2 is shown as an example.

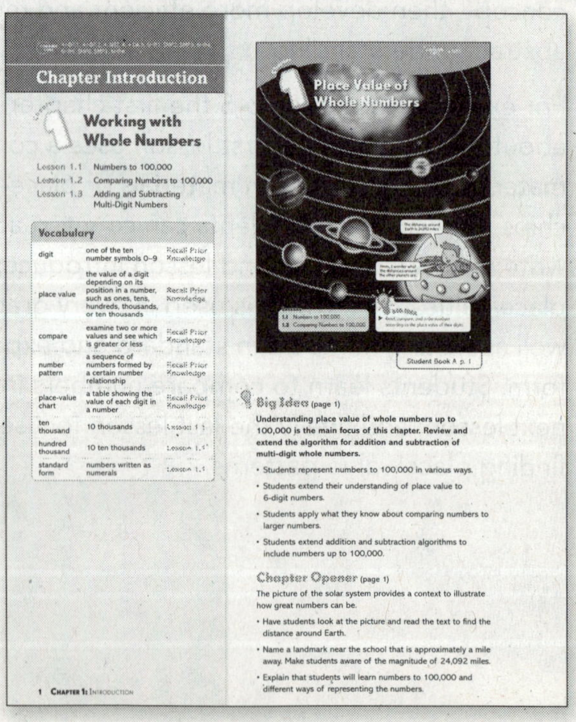

Chapter Introduction

Chapter 1 Working with Whole Numbers

Lesson 1.1 Numbers to 100,000
Lesson 1.2 Comparing Numbers to 100,000
Lesson 1.3 Adding and Subtracting Multi-Digit Numbers

Vocabulary		
digit	one of the ten number symbols 0–9	Recall Prior Knowledge
place value	the value of a digit depending on its position in a number, such as ones, tens, hundreds, thousands, or ten thousands	Recall Prior Knowledge
compare	examine two or more values and see which is greater or less	Recall Prior Knowledge
number pattern	a sequence of numbers formed by a certain number relationship	Recall Prior Knowledge
place-value chart	a table showing the value of each digit in a number	Recall Prior Knowledge
ten thousand	10 thousands	Lesson 1.1
hundred thousand	10 ten thousands	Lesson 1.1
standard form	numbers written as numerals	Lesson 1.1

Student Book A p. 1

Big Idea (page 1)

Understanding place value of whole numbers up to 100,000 is the main focus of this chapter. Review and extend the algorithm for addition and subtraction of multi-digit whole numbers.

- Students represent numbers to 100,000 in various ways.
- Students extend their understanding of place value to 6-digit numbers.
- Students apply what they know about comparing numbers to larger numbers.
- Students extend addition and subtraction algorithms to include numbers up to 100,000.

Chapter Opener (page 1)

The picture of the solar system provides a context to illustrate how great numbers can be.

- Have students look at the picture and read the text to find the distance around Earth.
- Name a landmark near the school that is approximately a mile away. Make students aware of the magnitude of 24,092 miles.
- Explain that students will learn numbers to 100,000 and different ways of representing the numbers.

1 Chapter 1: Introduction

Grade 4 is shown as an example.

Recall Prior Knowledge and Quick Check

Before students begin a new chapter, you will need to ensure that they have the prerequisite knowledge to be successful in that chapter. To begin, use the Recall Prior Knowledge, found on the page after the Chapter Opener, to review material that was presented either in an earlier chapter or grade. Ask the questions provided to review the examples. By doing so, you are not giving them the information but rather checking how many students retained the information. It is natural for students to forget some of what they've learned, so this is an opportunity to stimulate them to remember. If some of the material is new, you will have to teach it now.

If students are struggling with the material, be sure to notice whether it is format, vocabulary, or content that causes the difficulty.

Finally on the first day, following the Chapter Opener and Recall Prior Knowledge, you will assign either the Quick Check or the pre-test from the Assessments book. The Quick Check is found in the Student Book, making it the more convenient choice, but the pre-test is a more in depth diagnostic tool and is tied to the Teacher's Guide to Transition.

The pre-test will tell you if students have the prior knowledge to be successful in the current chapter. If not, you will need the Teacher's Guide to Transition described on the next page. Be sure to see if there are patterns of errors in the pre-test because that can help you decide whether to include some additional support as you move into the chapter. For example, if a third grade student doesn't know "expanded form," he or she still could move into the chapter, but you would make a point of emphasizing this as you taught Chapter 1.

Teacher Tip:

After the Recall Prior Knowledge, give the pre-test from the Assessment book. Remember, it is not a pretest of the chapter's content, but of the prerequisite knowledge to be successful in the chapter.

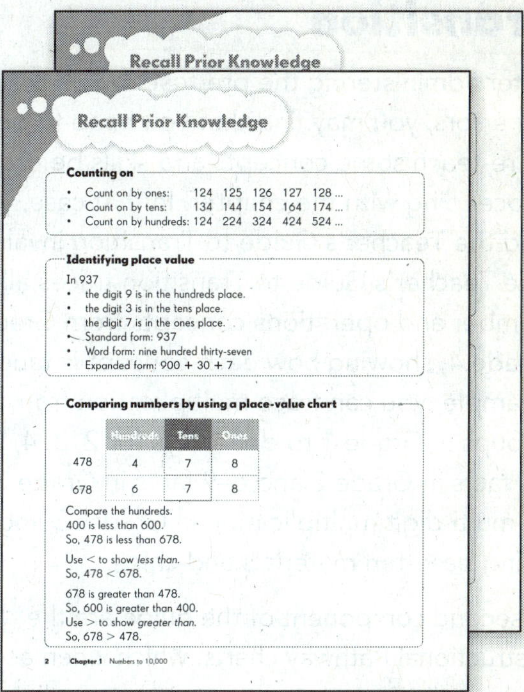

Recall Prior Knowledge

Counting on

- Count on by ones: 124 125 126 127 128 ...
- Count on by tens: 134 144 154 164 174 ...
- Count on by hundreds: 124 224 324 424 524 ...

Identifying place value

In 937
- the digit 9 is in the hundreds place.
- the digit 3 is in the tens place.
- the digit 7 is in the ones place.
- Standard form: 937
- Word form: nine hundred thirty-seven
- Expanded form: 900 + 30 + 7

Comparing numbers by using a place-value chart

	Hundreds	Tens	Ones
478	4	7	8
678	6	7	8

Compare the hundreds.
400 is less than 600.
So, 478 is less than 678.

Use < to show *less than*.
So, 478 < 678.

678 is greater than 478.
So, 600 is greater than 400.
Use > to show *greater than*.
So, 678 > 478.

2 Chapter 1 Numbers to 10,000

Grade 3 is shown as an example.

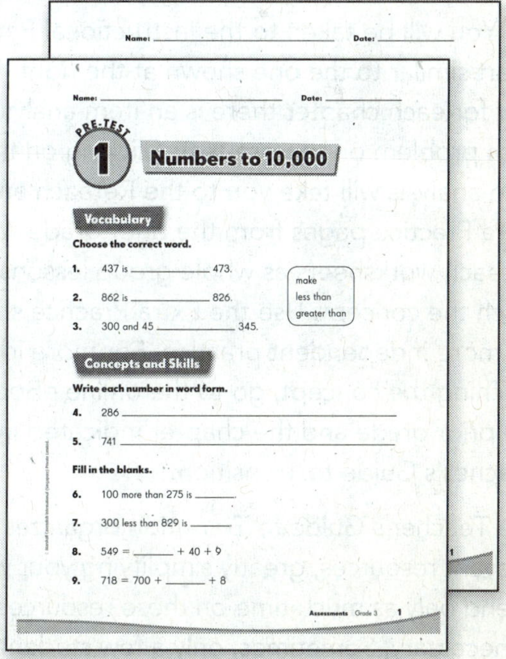

Name: Date:

PRE-TEST 1 **Numbers to 10,000**

Vocabulary

Choose the correct word.

1. 437 is ______ 473.
2. 862 is ______ 826.
3. 300 and 45 ______ 345.

make
less than
greater than

Concepts and Skills

Write each number in word form.

4. 286 ______
5. 741 ______

Fill in the blanks.

6. 100 more than 275 is ______.
7. 300 less than 829 is ______.
8. 549 = ______ + 40 + 9
9. 718 = 700 + ______ + 8

Assessments Grade 3 1

Grade 3 is shown as an example.

Use eBooks to see how a concept was taught in the prior grade. For instance, reviewing how subtraction was taught in Chapters 13 and 17 in Grade 1 can help when you teach subtraction in Chapter 3 in Grade 2.

Teacher's Guide to Transition

After administering the pre-test and analyzing it for errors, you may find that you need to go back to re-teach some concepts and skills before proceeding with the chapter. In that case, you will find the Teacher's Guide to Transition invaluable. The Teacher's Guide to Transition traces all the number and operations concepts from Grade 1 to Grade 4, showing how each concept is taught. For example, you can trace multiplication from simple groups in Grade 1 to dot arrays for 2, 3, 4, 5, and 10 facts in Grade 2 and 6–9 facts in Grade 3, then to multi-digit multiplication in Grades 3 and 4 using base-ten materials and chips.

A second component of the guide are the Instructional Pathway charts, which when accessed in the online version, can provide direct links to support resources. As you find weaknesses through administering the pre-test, go to the Instructional Pathway chart for the chapter you are working on. You will be taken to the Instructional Pathway Chart similar to the one shown at the right. Notice that for each chapter there is an item analysis for each problem on the pre-test. Clicking on the item analysis will take you to the Reteach and Extra Practice pages from the prior grade. Use the Reteach worksheets as whole group lessons to teach the concept. Use the Extra Practice sheets for more independent practice. For more ideas on teaching the concept, go to the online eBook for the prior grade and the chapter indicated in the Teacher's Guide to Transition.

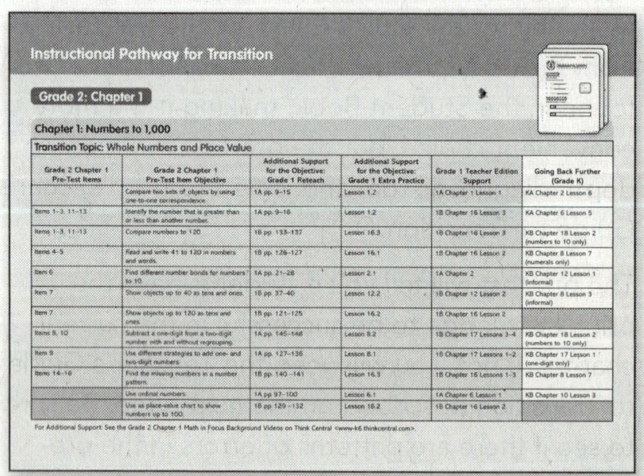

Instructional Pathway for Transition

Grade 2: Chapter 1

Chapter 1: Numbers to 1,000

Transition Topic: Whole Numbers and Place Value

Grade 2 Chapter 1 Pre-Test Items	Grade 2 Chapter 1 Pre-Test Item Objective	Additional Support for the Objective: Grade 1 Reteach	Additional Support for the Objective: Grade 1 Extra Practice	Grade 1 Teacher Edition Support	Going Back Further (Grade K)
	Compare two sets of objects by using one-to-one correspondence.	1A pp. 9–15	Lesson 1.2	1A Chapter 1 Lesson 1	KA Chapter 2 Lesson 6
Items 1–3, 11–13	Identify the number that is greater than or less than another number.	1A pp. 9–16	Lesson 1.2	1B Chapter 16 Lesson 3	KA Chapter 6 Lesson 5
Items 1–3, 11–13	Compare numbers to 120.	1B pp. 133–137	Lesson 16.3	1B Chapter 16 Lesson 3	KB Chapter 18 Lesson 2 (numbers to 10 only)
Items 4–5	Read and write 41 to 120 in numbers and words.	1B pp. 126–127	Lesson 16.1	1B Chapter 16 Lesson 2	KB Chapter 8 Lesson 7 (numerals only)
Item 6	Find different number bonds for numbers to 10.	1A pp. 21–28	Lesson 2.1	1A Chapter 2	KB Chapter 12 Lesson 1 (informal)
Item 7	Show objects up to 40 as tens and ones.	1B pp. 37–40	Lesson 12.2	1B Chapter 12 Lesson 2	KB Chapter 8 Lesson 3 (informal)
Item 7	Show objects up to 120 as tens and ones.	1B pp. 121–125	Lesson 16.2	1B Chapter 16 Lesson 2	
Items 8, 10	Subtract a one-digit from a two-digit number with and without regrouping.	1A pp. 145–148	Lesson 8.2	1B Chapter 17 Lessons 3–4	KB Chapter 18 Lesson 2 (numbers to 10 only)
Item 9	Use different strategies to add one- and two-digit numbers.	1A pp. 127–136	Lesson 8.1	1B Chapter 17 Lessons 1–2	KB Chapter 17 Lesson 1 (one-digit only)
Items 14–16	Find the missing numbers in a number pattern.	1B pp. 140–141	Lesson 16.3	1B Chapter 16 Lessons 1–3	KB Chapter 8 Lesson 7
	Use ordinal numbers.	1A pp. 97–100	Lesson 6.1	1A Chapter 6 Lesson 1	KB Chapter 10 Lesson 3
	Use as place-value chart to show numbers up to 100.	1B pp. 129–132	Lesson 16.2	1B Chapter 16 Lesson 2	

For Additional Support: See the Grade 2 Chapter 1 Math in Focus Background Videos on Think Central <www-k6.thinkcentral.com>.

The Teacher's Guide to Transition organizes the relevant resources, greatly simplifying your work. Spend only as much time on these resources as necessary. Sometimes, only a few students might need the support, other times it will be the whole class.

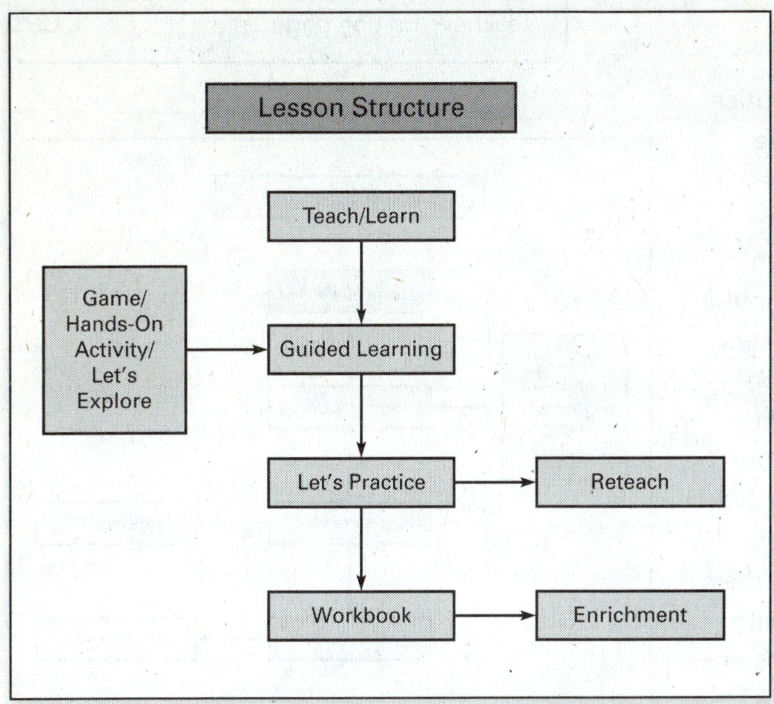

Lesson Structure for all *Math in Focus* Lessons

All *Math in Focus* lessons share the same structure, which is shown in the diagram above. Each part of the lesson will be discussed in more detail on the following pages.

Each lesson begins with a whole group lesson or mini-lesson called "Teach" in the Teacher's Edition and "Learn" in the Student Book. It is suggested that the student book should be closed during this portion.

Next comes the Guided Learning, or gradual release of responsibility to the student. This can be done with the whole group or with small groups by ability or to accommodate Response to Intervention (RtI). Students can also work with partners with teacher support.

Usually there is another Teach/Learn lesson and then another Guided Learning if the lesson has multiple objectives.

The Games, Let's Explore, and Hands-On Activities can be used in conjunction with Guided Learning to allow you to differentiate instruction and work in small groups.

Let's Practice is the independent practice done in the classroom that allows you to see whether students are ready to work independently in the Workbook. It is formative assessment and should be used to guide remediation or additional instruction.

If students are unsuccessful in Let's Practice, they will need to use the Reteach materials. If successful in Let's Practice, students are ready for the Workbook. Students can do one page in class and one or two pages at home for homework depending on the length of your math period.

If the homework pages are too easy, the students can be assigned pages from the Enrichment book. These are challenging problems on the same topic.

Lesson Planning

Teacher Tip:

Students should keep their book closed during Teach/Learn; they can go back later to review. Use sticky notes to write good questions for the Teach/Learn lesson, and keep them right on the Teacher's Edition page.

Teach/Learn

Now you are ready to teach the lessons. Notice that the first page of the lesson includes the necessary vocabulary and materials and then describes a whole group lesson. It is called "Teach" in the Teacher's Edition and "Learn" In the Student Book. The Student Books should be closed at this point because all the answers are on the page. Teach/Learn is meant to be an active component. The Teacher's Edition gives instructions on what to do and what the dialogue might look like. Students should have manipulatives—interlocking cubes, base-ten materials, fraction strips, etc.—as shown in the picture for the lesson. Students can work with partners or individually as you ask questions or model the concept. You will need to decide how to display what is shown on the page. Some possibilities are to place the manipulatives on a rug or to display them on an overhead, document camera, or interactive whiteboard. Finally, think of the questions you will ask as you teach the lesson.

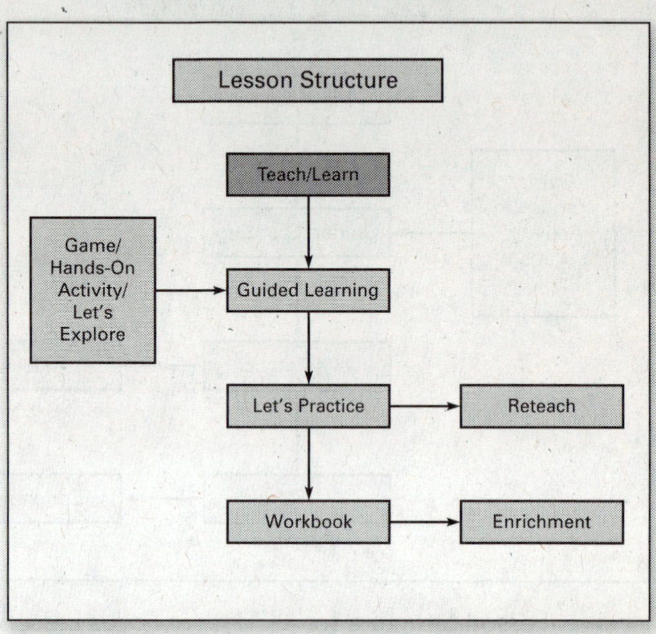

For example, in the lesson to the right from Chapter 1 in Grade 3, students are learning to read, write and understand numbers to 1,000. The student book should be closed as you direct the students to display 4 hundreds, 2 tens, and 5 ones, asking what number is represented. You ask the students how they know it is 425. Working with a partner, students next stack ten hundreds and count by hundreds, ending with one thousand. You can then ask how many hundreds make a thousand and write the answer on the board. Students might record something similar in a math journal. If necessary, you might repeat these activities with other numbers.

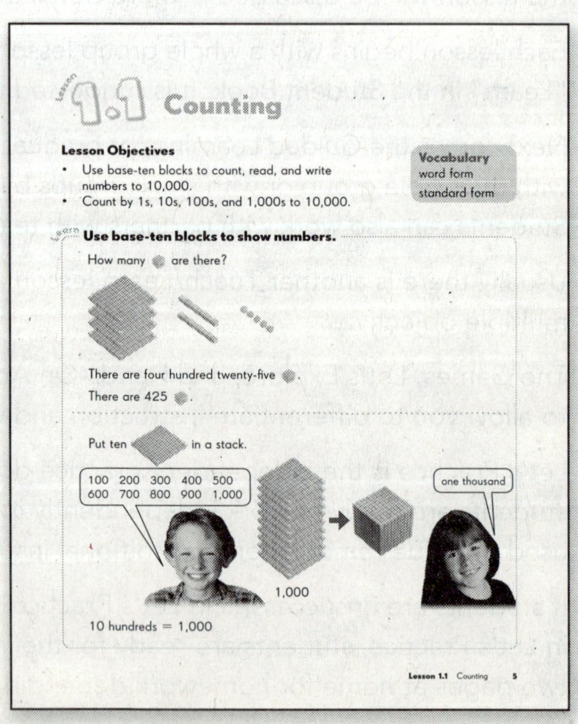

Lesson 1.1 Counting

Lesson Objectives

- Use base-ten blocks to count, read, and write numbers to 10,000.
- Count by 1s, 10s, 100s, and 1,000s to 10,000.

Vocabulary
word form
standard form

Learn **Use base-ten blocks to show numbers.**

How many are there?

There are four hundred twenty-five .

There are 425 .

Put ten in a stack.

100 200 300 400 500
600 700 800 900 1,000

one thousand

1,000

10 hundreds = 1,000

Lesson 1.1 Counting 5

Grade 3 is shown as an example.

Guided Learning

Immediately after the Teach/Learn lesson, you will see something called Guided Learning. Guided Learning is intended to provide practice for the students, but with teacher support. At first, this activity might be done with the whole class. The difference between Guided Learning and the Teach/Learn lesson is that you will ask questions more than model. You support the first few problems but then gradually release responsibility so students are trying them on their own. Guided Learning provides more examples for practice and indicates to you if your students are ready to work independently.

The Guided Learning contains problems similar to the Teach/Learn examples. You may see pictures of manipulatives in these problems. You will need to decide if students are ready for the pictorial representation or if they need to get out the materials. Sometimes the Guided Learning will be at the abstract level, and again you will need to assess whether students can work at that level or need a picture or concrete material.

In the example to the right, students are practicing writing standard and word form for numbers to 10,000 in Grade 3. Notice the first few problems include visual models, which students should be able to interpret. The rest of the problems are more abstract, asking students to convert from word form to standard form and vice versa. The idea is to help them with the first problems, but then see if students can do the rest of each set on their own. If they can, then you know that they understand the concept.

You may find that you can have some students work in pairs on the Guided Learning while you work with the remaining students.

Finally, notice that often there is another Teach/Learn lesson and Guided Learning that follows.

Teacher Tip:

If you know you will be doing another whole group Teach/Learn Lesson, you may want to have students keep their books closed during Guided Learning. You can write or project the problems.

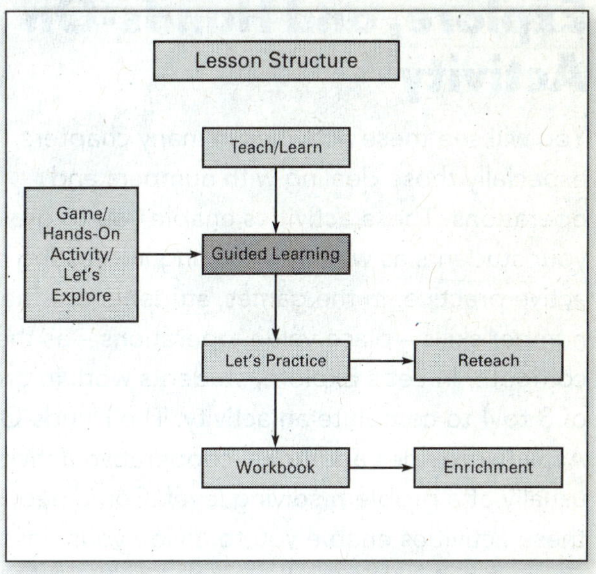

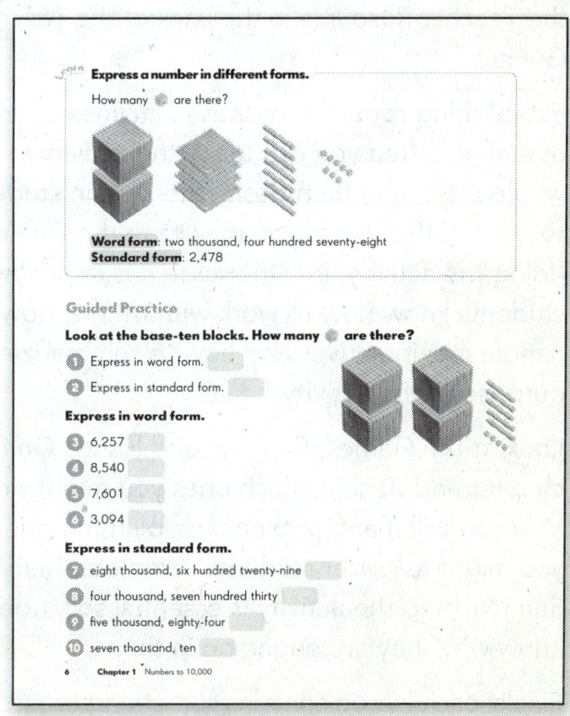
Express a number in different forms.

How many are there?

Word form: two thousand, four hundred seventy-eight
Standard form: 2,478

Guided Practice

Look at the base-ten blocks. How many are there?

1. Express in word form.
2. Express in standard form.

Express in word form.

3. 6,257
4. 8,540
5. 7,601
6. 3,094

Express in standard form.

7. eight thousand, six hundred twenty-nine
8. four thousand, seven hundred thirty
9. five thousand, eighty-four
10. seven thousand, ten

6 Chapter 1 Numbers to 10,000

Grade 3 is shown as an example.

Teacher Tip:

You can use any of these activities as centers in addition to using them to differentiate instruction.

Activities: Games, Let's Explore, and Hands-On Activity

You will see these activities in many chapters, especially those dealing with numbers and operations. These activities enable you to group your students as well as providing interesting and active practice. In the games, students use their number skills – place value, operations – as they compete. In Let's Explore, students work in groups of 3 to 4 to complete an activity. The Hands-On Activity provides additional cooperative activities, usually at a problem-solving level. Combined, these activities enable you to divide your class so you can teach a small group while the other students are doing the activity.

In general you will find that the games and activities do not involve many parts or pieces. When a board or number cards are necessary, they are available in the Teacher Resource in the back of the Teacher's Guide.

Establishing routines for these activities is essential. Often you can teach the activity to the whole class, and then designate certain students to do it. Other times you may have the whole class doing the activity. In either case it is important that students know how to work with others, how to handle manipulatives and how to summarize the purpose of the activity.

Look at the Games, Explore, and Hands On in the chapter and decide which ones you might do. Plan how you will manage them and plan the questions you might ask after students complete them. Summarizing the activity is essential so students know why they are engaging in them.

Finally each lesson contains something called Problem of the Lesson. You can use these as warm-ups or exit tickets after you have taught the lesson.

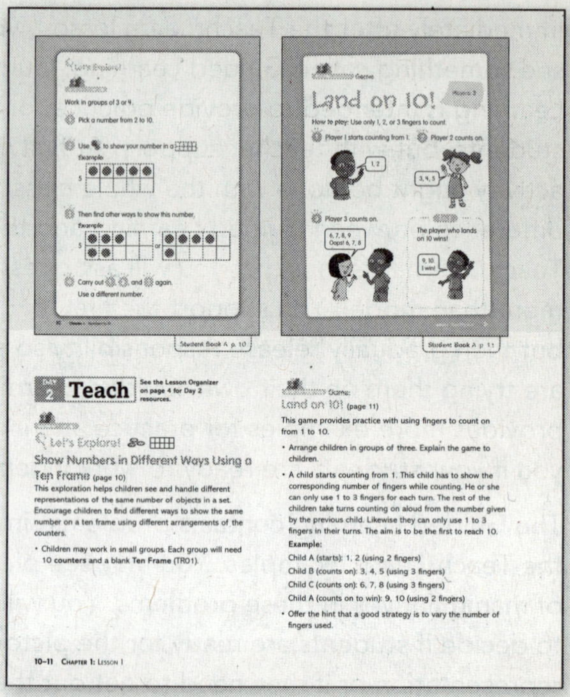

Student Book A p. 10

Student Book A p. 11

Day 2 **Teach** See the Lesson Organizer on page 4 for Day 2 resources.

Let's Explore!

Show Numbers in Different Ways Using a Ten Frame (page 10)

This exploration helps children see and handle different representations of the same number of objects in a set. Encourage children to find different ways to show the same number on a ten frame using different arrangements of the counters.

- Children may work in small groups. Each group will need 10 **counters** and a blank **Ten Frame** (TR01).

Game:

Land on 10! (page 11)

This game provides practice with using fingers to count on from 1 to 10.

- Arrange children in groups of three. Explain the game to children.
- A child starts counting from 1. This child has to show the corresponding number of fingers while counting. He or she can only use 1 to 3 fingers for each turn. The rest of the children take turns counting on aloud from the number given by the previous child. Likewise they can only use 1 to 3 fingers in their turns. The aim is to be the first to reach 10.

Example:

Child A (starts): 1, 2 (using 2 fingers)
Child B (counts on): 3, 4, 5 (using 3 fingers)
Child C (counts on): 6, 7, 8 (using 3 fingers)
Child A (counts on to win): 9, 10 (using 2 fingers)

- Offer the hint that a good strategy is to vary the number of fingers used.

10–11 Chapter 1: Lesson 1

Grade 1 is shown as an example.

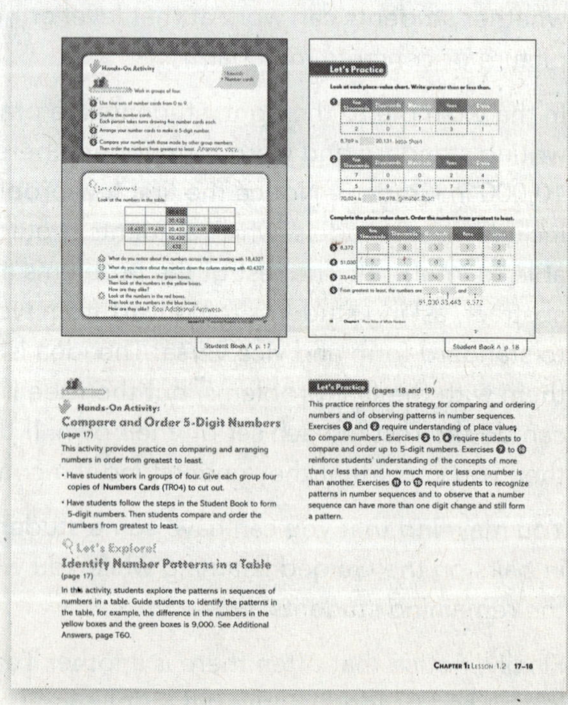

Student Book A p. 17

Student Book A p. 18

Hands-On Activity:

Compare and Order 5-Digit Numbers (page 17)

This activity provides practice on comparing and arranging numbers in order from greatest to least.

- Have students work in groups of four. Give each group four copies of **Numbers Cards** (TR04) to cut out.
- Have students follow the steps in the Student Book to form 5-digit numbers. Then students compare and order the numbers from greatest to least.

Let's Explore!

Identify Number Patterns in a Table (page 17)

In this activity, students explore the patterns in sequences of numbers in a table. Guide students to identify the patterns in the table, for example, the difference in the numbers in the yellow boxes and the green boxes is 9,000. See Additional Answers, page T60.

Let's Practice (pages 18 and 19)

This practice reinforces the strategy for comparing and ordering numbers and of observing patterns in number sequences. Exercises 1 and 2 require understanding of place values to compare numbers. Exercises 3 to 6 require students to compare and order up to 5-digit numbers. Exercises 7 to 10 reinforce students' understanding of the concepts of more than or less than and how much more or less one number is than another. Exercises 11 to [illegible] require students to recognize patterns in number sequences and to observe that a number sequence can have more than one digit change and still form a pattern.

Chapter 1: Lesson 1.2 17–18

Grade 4 is shown as an example.

Teacher Tip:

In primary grades, have students number their notebooks or whiteboards before trying the Let's Practice. Feel free to read the problems. In all grades, circulate to see if students are demonstrating mastery or not.

Let's Practice: Independent Practice

After several rounds of whole group and guided practice, you should see the feature called Let's Practice. It will appear at the end of the lesson in either a one-day or multiple day lesson. Let's Practice is intended as formative assessment for you to decide if students are ready to work independently in the workbook. Students will need their books to do these. They number their paper or notebook and work independently on completing all of the problems. Notice that some problems contain visual models and others are abstract. The problems also increase in complexity. One problem may simply ask students what number has 3 tens and 5 ones and a couple of problems later it may ask "30 is __ tens and 10 ones" to see if students have really mastered the concept of ones and tens in first grade.

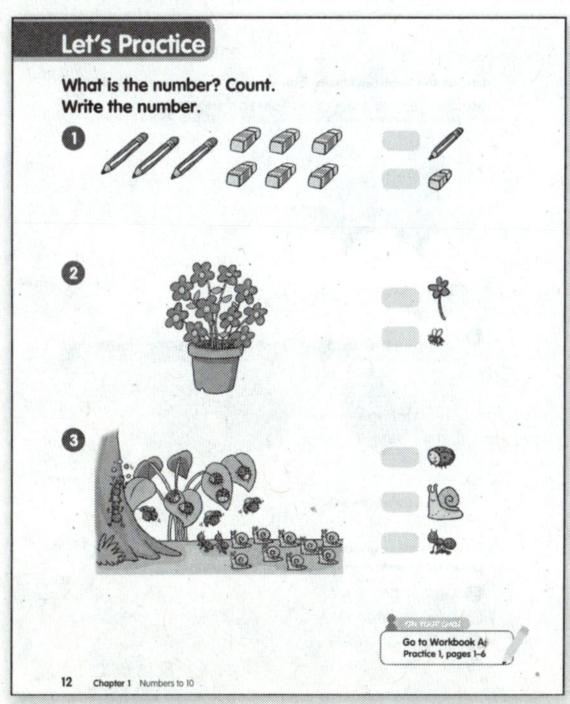

Let's Practice

What is the number? Count. Write the number.

1

2

3

ON YOUR OWN

Go to Workbook A: Practice 1, pages 1–6

12 Chapter 1 Numbers to 10

Grade 1 is shown as an example.

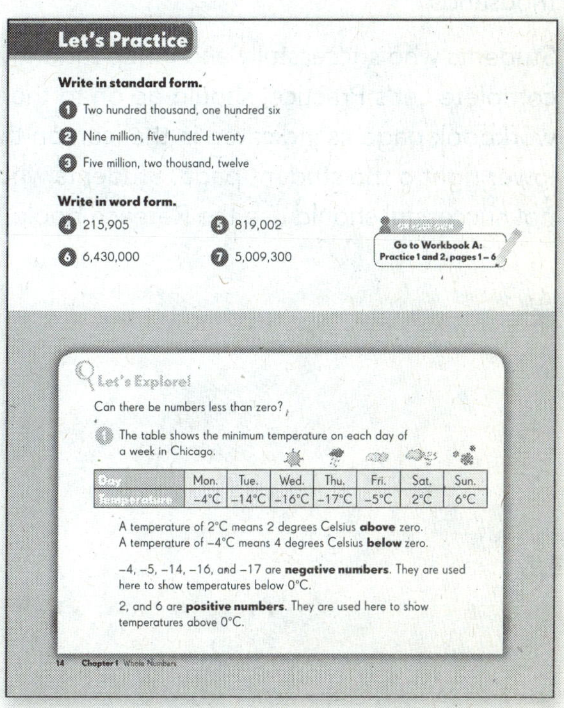

Let's Practice

Write in standard form.

1 Two hundred thousand, one hundred six

2 Nine million, five hundred twenty

3 Five million, two thousand, twelve

Write in word form.

4 215,905

5 819,002

6 6,430,000

7 5,009,300

ON YOUR OWN

Go to Workbook A: Practice 1 and 2, pages 1–6

Let's Explore!

Can there be numbers less than zero?

1 The table shows the minimum temperature on each day of a week in Chicago.

Day	Mon.	Tue.	Wed.	Thu.	Fri.	Sat.	Sun.
Temperature	–4°C	–14°C	–16°C	–17°C	–5°C	2°C	6°C

A temperature of 2°C means 2 degrees Celsius **above** zero.
A temperature of –4°C means 4 degrees Celsius **below** zero.

–4, –5, –14, –16, and –17 are **negative numbers**. They are used here to show temperatures below 0°C.

2, and 6 are **positive numbers**. They are used here to show temperatures above 0°C.

14 Chapter 1 Whole Numbers

Grade 5 is shown as an example.

In the primary grades you can use individual white boards as well as notebooks or other paper. Students can't write in their books, so the first few times you will have to model how to number and record answers. Dividing a small white board into 4 quadrants and numbering it 1-4 on the front and 5-8 on the back is helpful.

In all the grades, be sure to circulate. If students are struggling, you can stop this activity or limit the ones the student needs to do. Remember, the purpose for this activity is for you to get a good sense of how many students are ready to work independently and on what topics. Look for patterns of errors to know what to re-teach.

In the sample from 3rd grade, students first must be able to understand pictorial models of numbers in the thousands, then use their knowledge of place value to determine the numbers in a pattern based on increasing either ones, tens, hundreds or thousands.

Students who successfully and independently complete Let's Practice, should go on to the workbook page as indicated in the icon on the lower right o the student page. Students who are not successful should use the Reteach book.

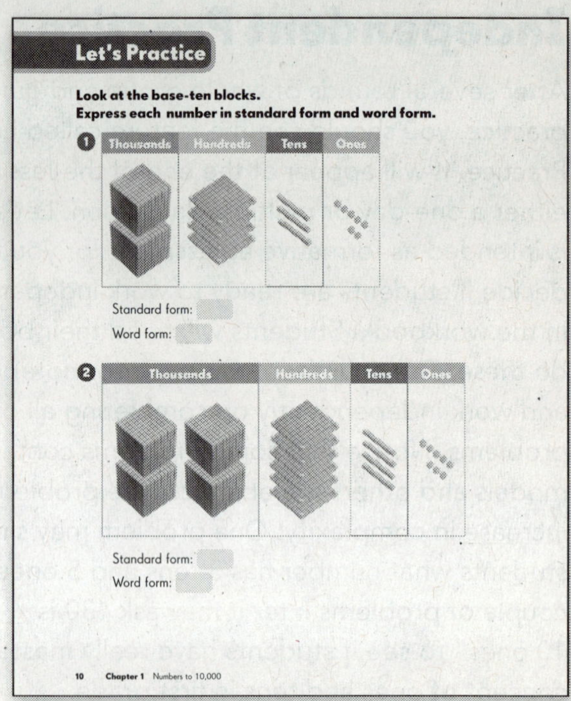

Let's Practice

Look at the base-ten blocks.
Express each number in standard form and word form.

1 Thousands | Hundreds | Tens | Ones

Standard form:
Word form:

2 Thousands | Hundreds | Tens | Ones

Standard form:
Word form:

10 **Chapter 1** Numbers to 10,000

Grade 3 is shown as an example.

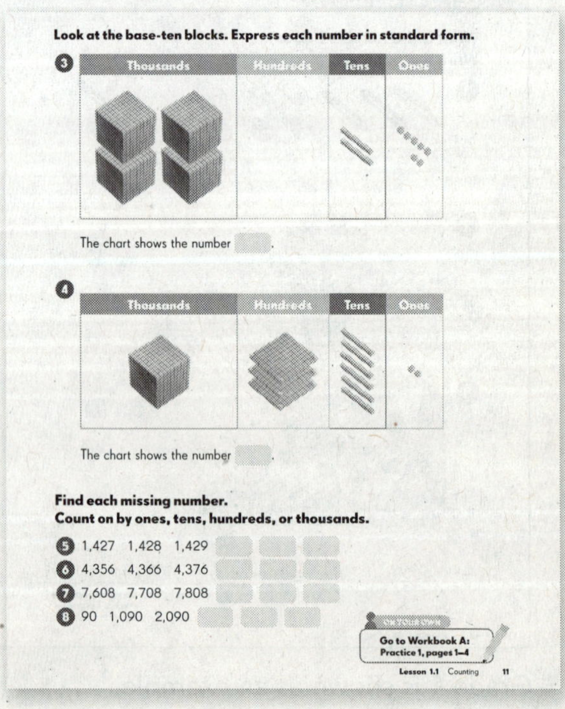

Look at the base-ten blocks. Express each number in standard form.

3 Thousands | Hundreds | Tens | Ones

The chart shows the number .

4 Thousands | Hundreds | Tens | Ones

The chart shows the number .

Find each missing number.
Count on by ones, tens, hundreds, or thousands.

5 1,427 1,428 1,429
6 4,356 4,366 4,376
7 7,608 7,708 7,808
8 90 1,090 2,090

Go to Workbook A: Practice 1, pages 1–4

Lesson 1.1 Counting 11

Grade 3 is shown as an example.

Teacher Tip:

Since the first page of every workbook assignment contains a worked out example, you may want to use that for homework and do the next page in class.

Workbook: Independent Practice

Look for the workbook pages at the end of Lesson 1. You should see 4 or more sheets. These worksheets are intended to be done both in class as independent practice and as homework pages. Usually you will assign one in class and one or two to take home. Students should NOT be doing the workbook pages until they can successfully do them. The purpose of these pages is to practice and become fluent, not to learn. That is why they are assigned only after the student demonstrates competence in the Let's Practice.

The workbook pages parallel the work done in Teach/Learn and Guided Learning. Most pages begin with examples that use pictorial models, then include more abstract questions. Primary grades have lots of pictorial models so there is a minimum of reading. Students should be familiar with the questions, but you may have to go over them before sending them home. Check for understanding before they take them home.

You will also notice there are sometimes as many as 5 or 6 worksheets. That is because the next lessons are usually multiple day lessons and there won't be independent practice for the first day. You can use the workbook pages from the previous lesson so students continue to practice at home.

The key to the workbook pages is to make sure students are able to do them before assigning them. If students are struggling you may need to give them the Reteach or Extra Practice worksheets. Notice how the first grade sheets above include an example so parents will understand what is being asked of the student.

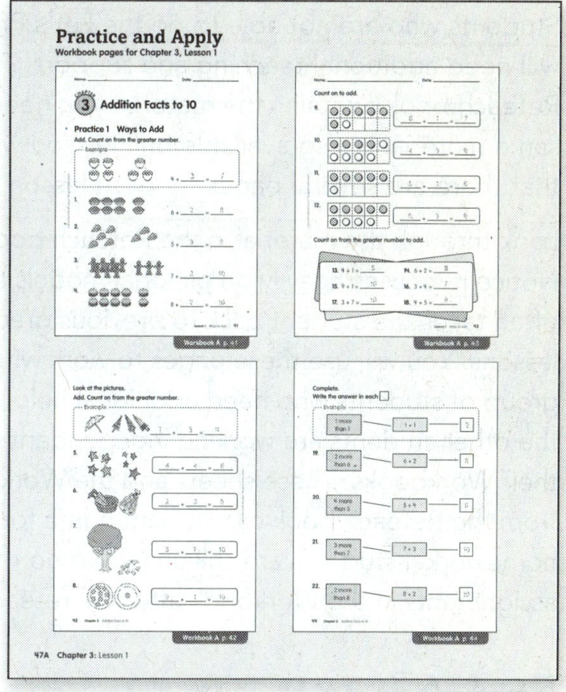

Grade 1 is shown as an example.

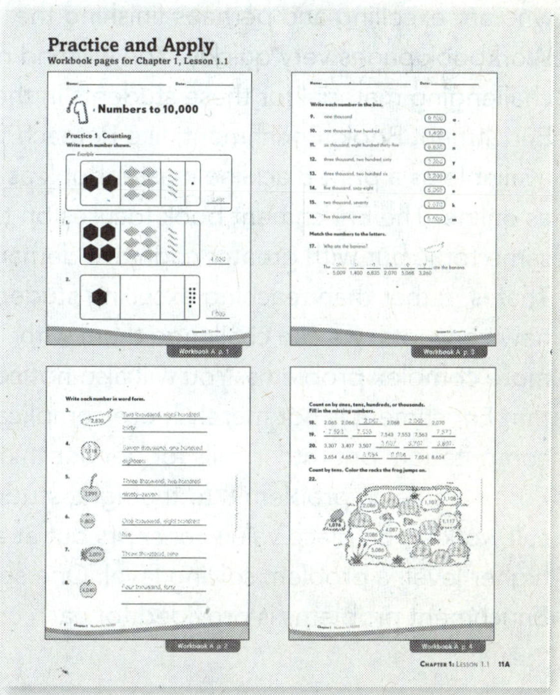

Grade 3 is shown as an example.

Reteach

Students who are not able to do the Let's Practice will need additional teaching and support. The Reteach book contains the material you need. The same material is also available online. You will see that there are several pages for each lesson.

Look through the material in the Reteach book. Notice it focuses heavily on pictorial models and often takes the student back to previous grades or lessons. You will use these pages to work with the group of students who need additional help, while the other students are working independently in their Workbooks. These sheets and the Worksheets from the Reteach book can be sent home for homework if students are still unable to do the assignments in the Workbook after the reteaching.

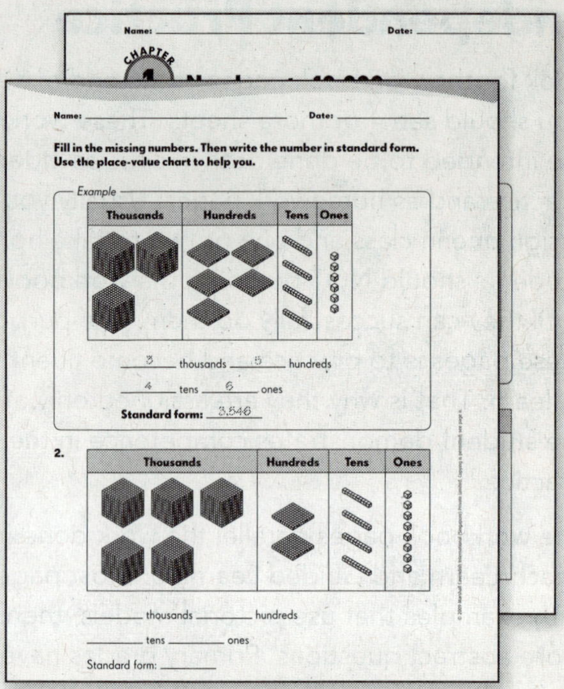

Name: ______ Date: ______

Fill in the missing numbers. Then write the number in standard form. Use the place-value chart to help you.

Example

Thousands	Hundreds	Tens	Ones

3 thousands 5 hundreds

4 tens 6 ones

Standard form: 3,546

2.

Thousands	Hundreds	Tens	Ones

______ thousands ______ hundreds

______ tens ______ ones

Standard form: ______

Grade 3 is shown as an example.

Enrichment

On the other hand, you probably have students who are excelling and perhaps finishing the Workbook pages very quickly. You will find more challenging material for these students in the Enrichment Book. Enrichment, like Reteach, is available as a print Blackline master book as well as online. The Enrichment book focuses on the same topic but with greater cognitive demands. That is, rather than teaching excelling students new concepts, we can challenge them with more complex problems. You will also notice that Enrichment is not merely more complicated computation, but rather calls for deeper thinking. For example, in problem 8 to the right, students are still working on place value concepts but at a much higher level: a problem solving level. One set of Enrichment problems is provided for each chapter.

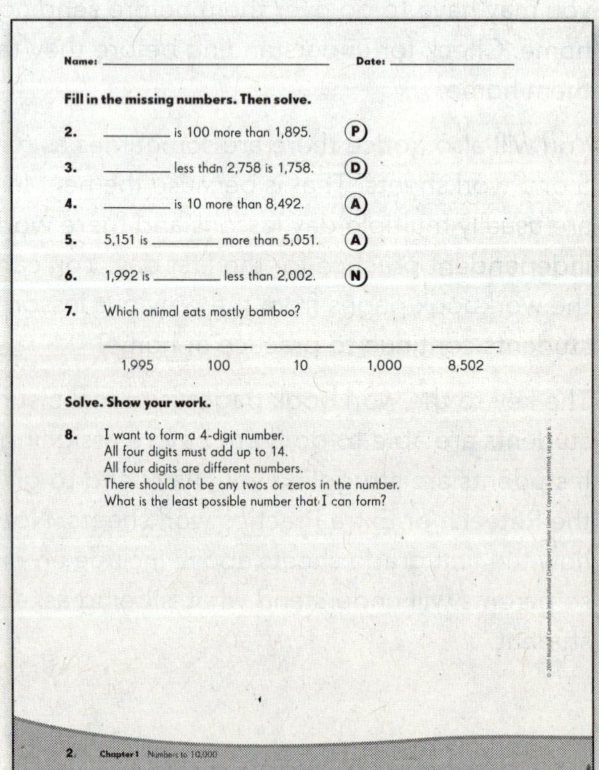

Name: ______ Date: ______

Fill in the missing numbers. Then solve.

2. ______ is 100 more than 1,895. (P)

3. ______ less than 2,758 is 1,758. (D)

4. ______ is 10 more than 8,492. (A)

5. 5,151 is ______ more than 5,051. (A)

6. 1,992 is ______ less than 2,002. (N)

7. Which animal eats mostly bamboo?

______ ______ ______ ______ ______

1,995 100 10 1,000 8,502

Solve. Show your work.

8. I want to form a 4-digit number.
All four digits must add up to 14.
All four digits are different numbers.
There should not be any twos or zeros in the number.
What is the least possible number that I can form?

2 Chapter 1 Numbers to 10,000

Grade 3 is shown as an example.

Additional Chapter Features

Teacher Tip:

Don't skip the Put on Your Thinking Cap! problems. These problems embody the framework of putting problem solving at the heart of teaching math.

Put on Your Thinking Cap! and Math Journal

Besides solving, students also need repeated opportunities to solve non-routine problems, which require students to synthesize the concepts, skills, and strategies they have acquired. This type of problem, labeled Put on Your Thinking Cap! is found at the end of every chapter. Students can work on these problems independently or in small groups. Your role is to encourage persistence, to ask guiding questions, and to help students summarize solutions and strategies. Several different problem solving strategies are suggested in the Teacher's Edition; use these as needed to guide students to think about which strategy works best for them in this situation. The Workbook contains two or three additional Put on Your Thinking Cap! problems that can be done in class and as homework.

As you begin, think of questions to help students get started without revealing the whole answer. After students have completed the problems, summarize the solutions so students can apply them in the Workbook problems. If students work in groups of two or four, model how students should work together. Remember, the focus of these problems is the thinking necessary to solve them, not just the solutions.

The Math Journal encourages students to explain their thinking through writing and to see that math is about thinking and reasoning. Often the Math Journal will model what a good answer might look like. Be sure to review this model with your students.

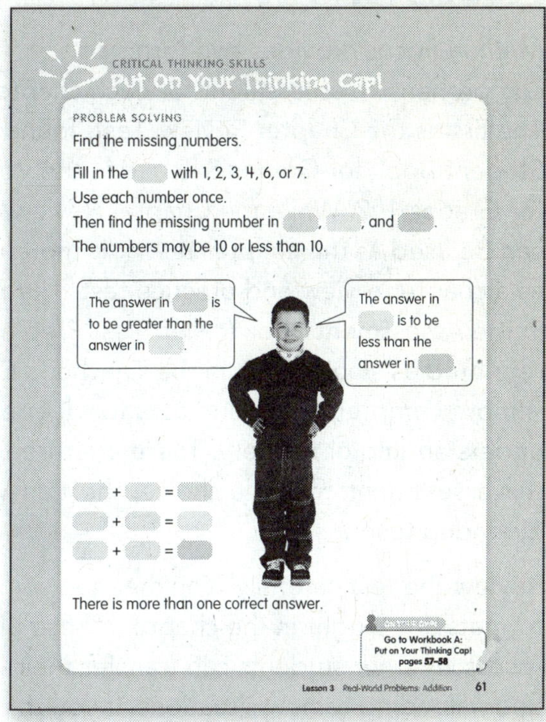
CRITICAL THINKING SKILLS
Put on Your Thinking Cap!

PROBLEM SOLVING

Find the missing numbers.

Fill in the ▢ with 1, 2, 3, 4, 6, or 7.
Use each number once.
Then find the missing number in ▢, ▢, and ▢.
The numbers may be 10 or less than 10.

The answer in ▢ is to be greater than the answer in ▢.

The answer in ▢ is to be less than the answer in ▢.

▢ + ▢ = ▢
▢ + ▢ = ▢
▢ + ▢ = ▢

There is more than one correct answer.

Go to Workbook A: Put on Your Thinking Cap! pages 57–58

Lesson 3 Real-World Problems: Addition 61

Grade 1 is shown as an example.

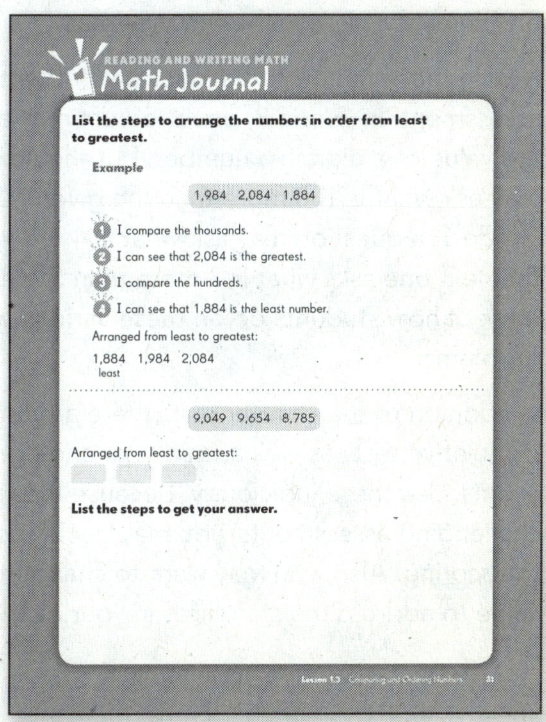
READING AND WRITING MATH
Math Journal

List the steps to arrange the numbers in order from least to greatest.

Example

1,984 2,084 1,884

1. I compare the thousands.
2. I can see that 2,084 is the greatest.
3. I compare the hundreds.
4. I can see that 1,884 is the least number.

Arranged from least to greatest:

1,884 1,984 2,084
least

9,049 9,654 8,785

Arranged from least to greatest:

▢ ▢ ▢

List the steps to get your answer.

Grade 3 is shown as an example.

Teacher Tip:

Put stars next to the problems you think will really test students. Explain to students that there will be challenging problems, some of which they may not have seen before, but they have the skills to solve them.

Assessment

Math in Focus provides two forms of comprehensive assessment for each chapter. The first is the Chapter Review/Test, found in the Student Book for Grades 3–5 and in the Workbook for Grades 1–2. While the Chapter Review/Test can be used as the chapter test, it is more useful as a chapter review and practice test. The test in the Assessment book (called Test Prep and reprinted as small pages in the Teacher's Edition) is more comprehensive and asks for deeper understanding or mastery. There are three parts to this assessment: multiple choice, short answer, and extended response.

Review the test carefully. You may see some formats not taught in the chapter. These questions assess whether students can transfer their understanding to new situations. If you think some of these questions are too difficult, give them as extra credit questions. Students who can do these problems are demonstrating true mastery.

Notice the variation in the kinds of problems in the assessment. In Grade 3, one problem may ask for the value of a digit in a number, but the next item may ask what is 100 more than the given number. In Grade 1, a question may ask what is 4 + 3 while the next one asks what is 3 more than 5. Keeping track of how students do on these various types of problems.

In addition to the chapter tests there are 6 to 8 cumulative tests as well as mid-year and end-of-year exams. Use these judiciously. Because these are challenging assessments, you may decide to adjust the scoring. Also, you may want to change the point value to address the standards in your district.

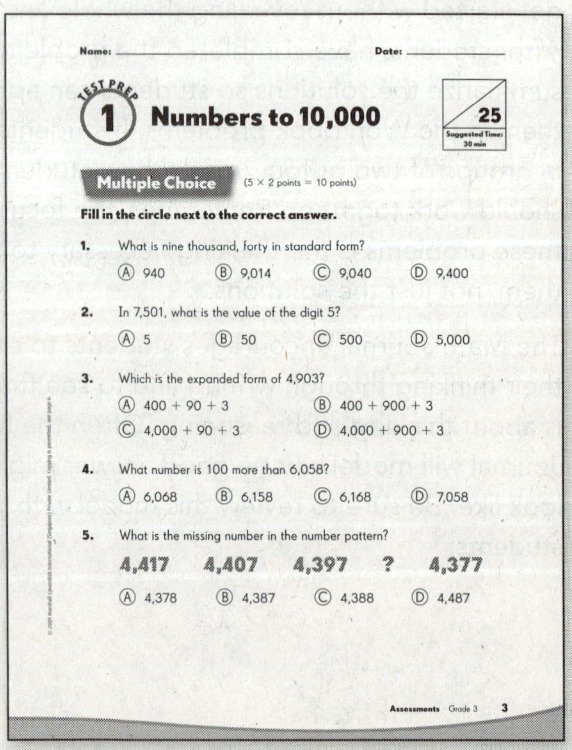

Name: Date:

TEST PREP 1 **Numbers to 10,000**

25 Suggested Time: 30 min

Multiple Choice (5 × 2 points = 10 points)

Fill in the circle next to the correct answer.

1. What is nine thousand, forty in standard form?
   Ⓐ 940 Ⓑ 9,014 Ⓒ 9,040 Ⓓ 9,400
2. In 7,501, what is the value of the digit 5?
   Ⓐ 5 Ⓑ 50 Ⓒ 500 Ⓓ 5,000
3. Which is the expanded form of 4,903?
   Ⓐ 400 + 90 + 3 Ⓑ 400 + 900 + 3
   Ⓒ 4,000 + 90 + 3 Ⓓ 4,000 + 900 + 3
4. What number is 100 more than 6,058?
   Ⓐ 6,068 Ⓑ 6,158 Ⓒ 6,168 Ⓓ 7,058
5. What is the missing number in the number pattern?
   4,417 4,407 4,397 ? 4,377
   Ⓐ 4,378 Ⓑ 4,387 Ⓒ 4,388 Ⓓ 4,487

Assessments Grade 3 3

Grade 4 is shown as an example.

Concrete to Pictorial to Abstract Pedagogy

Teacher Tip:

Make sure you have an efficient system of distributing and collecting manipulatives, whether in baskets, zip-top bags, or some other way, so that you can quickly begin the lesson.

At the heart of *Math In Focus* is the remarkably effective pedagogy of starting from concrete materials, then connecting these materials to pictorial representations, and finally visualizing those representations when solving problems abstractly. The goal is to develop abstract understanding. This sequence is not linear but moves fluidly back and forth, providing enough concrete experiences to develop conceptual understanding, and enough visual models to enable abstract fluency. Much of this pedagogy stems from the work of Jerome Bruner, whom the Singapore Math authors cite often. Bruner explained that students could do very abstract reasoning and even problem solving if they had a material to act it out with. He also explained the importance of visualization in developing understanding.

Let's look at some examples. In Grade 1, students use number bonds and ten frames to develop an understanding of adding and subtracting quantities to 20. The number bond is a visual model for showing part-part-whole relationships. Students begin with interlocking cubes and divide them into two quantities. They put the cubes into the number bond framework and then assign numbers for the parts and the whole. Eventually, we want students to be able to visualize these number bonds when performing simple operations. Similarly, the ten frames are used to organize quantities so they are easily recognizable without counting. Students learn to build 5 on top, some on the bottom, and memorize the number of empty spaces. In that way, when they are adding numbers whose sum is greater than 10, they can always fill in the first number to ten, and then add the rest. In other words, 8 + 4 = 8 + 2 + 2. If done abstractly, some students might not understand this, but when done with cubes and ten frames it becomes accessible to all students.

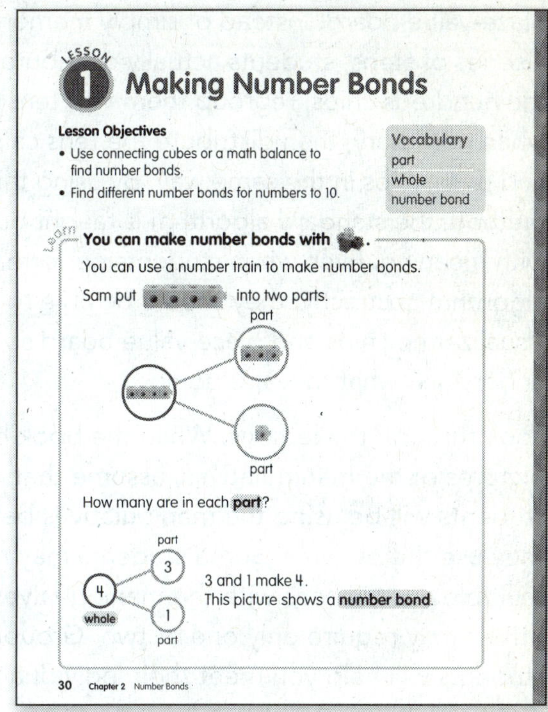

LESSON 1 Making Number Bonds

Lesson Objectives
- Use connecting cubes or a math balance to find number bonds.
- Find different number bonds for numbers to 10.

Vocabulary
part
whole
number bond

Learn

You can make number bonds with .

You can use a number train to make number bonds.

Sam put into two parts.

part

part

How many are in each **part**?

part 3
4 whole
1 part

3 and 1 make 4.
This picture shows a **number bond**.

30 Chapter 2 Number Bonds

Grade 1 is shown as an example.

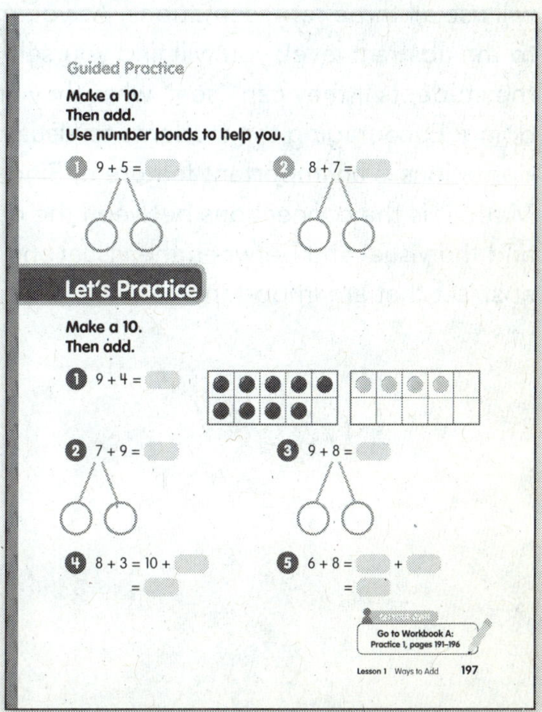

Guided Practice

Make a 10.
Then add.
Use number bonds to help you.

1. 9 + 5 =
2. 8 + 7 =

Let's Practice

Make a 10.
Then add.

1. 9 + 4 =
2. 7 + 9 =
3. 9 + 8 =
4. 8 + 3 = 10 +
 =
5. 6 + 8 = +
 =

Go to Workbook A: Practice 1, pages 191–196

Lesson 1 Ways to Add 197

Grade 1 is shown as an example.

In Grade 4, students learn the long division algorithm by using place-value chips on a place-value board. Instead of simply memorizing a series of steps, students actually distribute the hundreds chips, regroup them into tens when necessary, then distribute the tens chips and ones chips in the same way. By using this method, the standard algorithm is taught but with meaning. Even when students perform the algorithm abstractly, they should be able to visualize the chips and place-value board so they understand what they are doing.

Look through the lessons. While the book has pictures of the manipulatives, assume that students will be using the manipulatives before they use the pictures. Some students may require multiple experiences with the manipulatives, while others may require only one or two. Grouping students will help you meet their individual needs.

This sequence—concrete to pictorial to abstract—is used throughout *Math in Focus*. Most days you will use all three representations. As you move to the abstract level, you will find yourself asking the students if they can "see" what they are doing. Encouraging the students to visualize the operations is an important feature of Singapore Math. It is the connections between the concrete and the visual and between the visual and the abstract that are important.

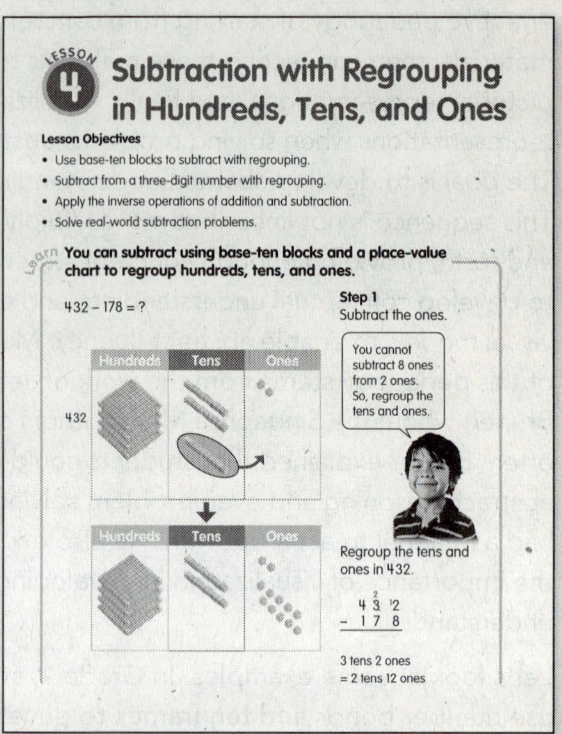
Lesson 4
Subtraction with Regrouping in Hundreds, Tens, and Ones

Lesson Objectives
- Use base-ten blocks to subtract with regrouping.
- Subtract from a three-digit number with regrouping.
- Apply the inverse operations of addition and subtraction.
- Solve real-world subtraction problems.

Learn **You can subtract using base-ten blocks and a place-value chart to regroup hundreds, tens, and ones.**

432 – 178 = ?

Step 1
Subtract the ones.

Regroup the tens and ones in 432.

$$\begin{array}{r} 4\,\overset{2}{\cancel{3}}\,{}^{1}2 \\ -\ 1\ 7\ 8 \\ \hline \end{array}$$

3 tens 2 ones
= 2 tens 12 ones

Grade 2 is shown as an example.

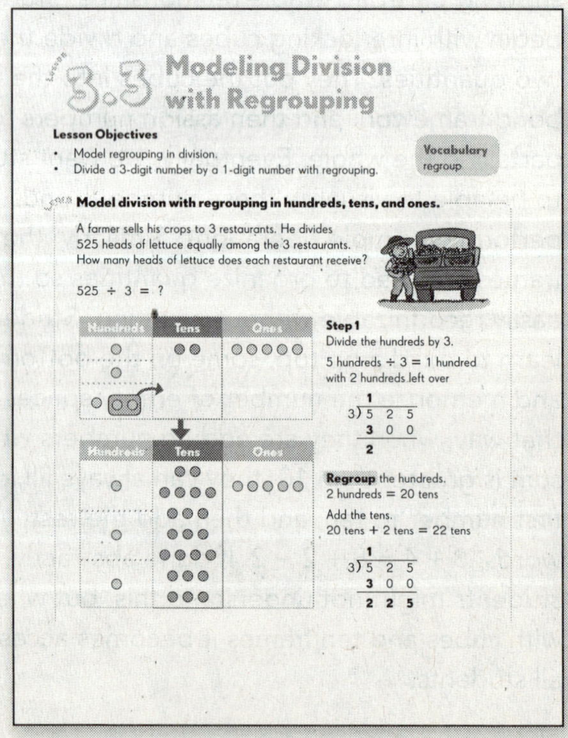
Lesson 3.3
Modeling Division with Regrouping

Lesson Objectives
- Model regrouping in division.
- Divide a 3-digit number by a 1-digit number with regrouping.

Vocabulary
regroup

Learn **Model division with regrouping in hundreds, tens, and ones.**

A farmer sells his crops to 3 restaurants. He divides 525 heads of lettuce equally among the 3 restaurants. How many heads of lettuce does each restaurant receive?

525 ÷ 3 = ?

Step 1
Divide the hundreds by 3.
5 hundreds ÷ 3 = 1 hundred with 2 hundreds left over

$$\begin{array}{r} 1 \\ 3\overline{)\,5\ 2\ 5} \\ 3\ 0\ 0 \\ \hline 2 \end{array}$$

Regroup the hundreds.
2 hundreds = 20 tens

Add the tens.
20 tens + 2 tens = 22 tens

$$\begin{array}{r} 1 \\ 3\overline{)\,5\ 2\ 5} \\ 3\ 0\ 0 \\ \hline 2\ 2\ 5 \end{array}$$

Grade 4 is shown as an example.

Technology Resources

By now you realize that you have a wealth of resources to teach all the students in your classroom. But increasingly, classrooms are also introducing new technology. *Math in Focus* includes a variety of technology resources to enhance the learning experience.

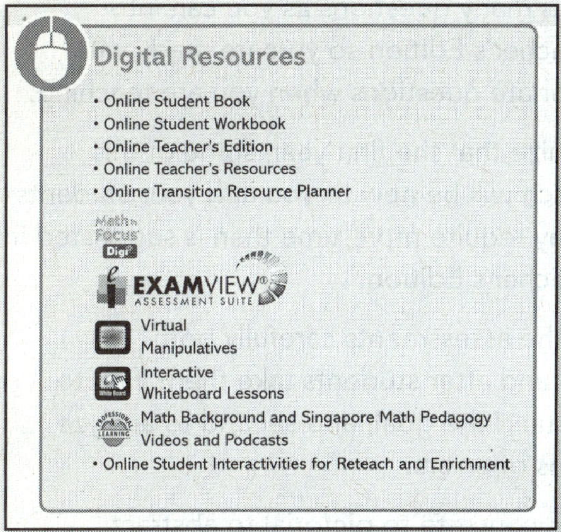

As part of the online Teacher's Resources you can access the following in printable PDF format:

- Reteach
- Enrichment
- Extra Practice
- Assessments
- School-to-Home Connections

Also available:

- Online Assessment Generator
- Lesson Planner
- Teacher's Guide to Transition with Instructional Pathway charts that link out to extra support resources.

One of the new features of Math in Focus is Math in Focus Digi+, which offers a full digital curriculum aligned to Math in Focus to use for each part of the lesson, including Teach, Guided Learning, Learn, Practice, and Assessment. Teachers can use Digi+ in the classroom for whole or small group instruction, or they can assign students lessons or activities within Digi+ to complete individually.

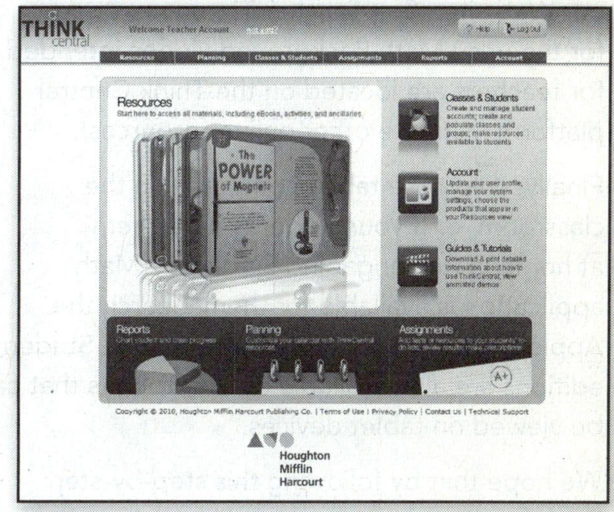

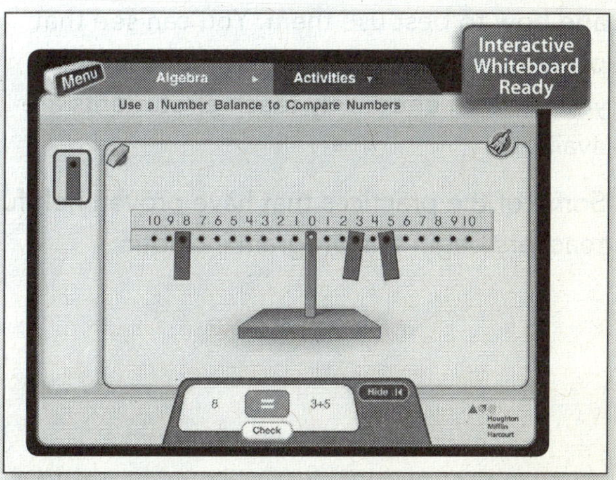

Teacher Tip:

If you have additional questions, visit the *Math in Focus* eLearning Web site at hmhelearning.com or our Web site at www.hmheducation.com/mathinfocus.

An Online Assessment Generator, Lesson Planner, and Online Teacher's Guide to Transition are also available. Each teacher and student will receive his or her own log-in information, so you can plan from home without having to bring the books home each day.

Additionally, videos and podcasts are available for teachers and parents to explain what we are teaching and why. When parents and teachers work together, students benefit enormously. These are located on our eLearning site and our Web site. (See Teacher Tip on next page for the urls.) Math Background videos intended for teachers are located on the Think Central platform (with the other online resources).

Finally, if you use tablet computers in the classroom, or if your students have them at home, a fun, engaging Singapore Math application is available for them. Search the Apple App store for "Singapore Math". Student editions are also available as eTextbooks that can be viewed on tablet devices.

We hope that by following this step-by-step implementation guide, you will have a more complete idea of the resources available to you and how to best use them. You can see that planning is required, but that the resources you need to effectively teach all students are available.

Some of the practices that have proven helpful as teachers begin this program include:

- Work with your fellow teachers to plan a chapter at a time, rather than a day or even week at a time.
- Write as many questions as you can into the Teacher's Edition so you are ready with appropriate questions when you are teaching.
- Recognize that the first year, some of this approach will be new to you and your students and may require more time than is suggested in the Teacher's Edition.
- Study the assessments carefully both before and after students take them, first to understand the goal, and second to analyze patterns of errors.
- Use the concrete to pictorial to abstract approach in daily lessons.
- Recognize the subtle differences as each lesson builds on the previous one, adding a new level of understanding.
- Teach for mastery.
- Most of all, enjoy the satisfaction you will feel when students say math is their favorite subject and they love solving problems.
- Finally, please join our online community on Facebook **https://www.facebook.com/HMHeducation**, Twitter, and our blog **www.singaporemathblog.com** to share with other educators using *Math in Focus*.

Notes:

Notes:

Notes:

Notes:

Notes:

Notes: